D1472789

Healthy Sexuality

What Is It?

By Julie K. Endersbe, MEd

Consultant:
Jennifer A. Oliphant, MPH
Research Fellow and Community Outreach Coordinator
National Teen Pregnancy Prevention Research Center
University of Minnesota

Perspectives on Relationships

LifeMatters
an imprint of Capstone Press
Mankato, Minnesota

LifeMatters books are published by Capstone Press
818 North Willow Street • Mankato, Minnesota 56001
http://www.capstone-press.com

Printed in the United States of America

Library of Congress Cataloging-in-Publication Data
Endersbe, Julie.
      Healthy sexuality : what is it? / by Julie Endersbe.
          p.   cm. — (Perspectives on healthy sexuality)
      Includes bibliographical references and index.
      ISBN 0-7368-0273-8 (book). — ISBN 0-7368-0293-2 (series)
      1. Sex. 2. Sex instruction for teenagers. 3. Sexual ethics. 4.
      Hygiene, Sexual. 5. Man-woman relationships. I. Title. II. Series:
      Endersbe, Julie. Perspectives on healthy sexuality.
      HQ21.E68 2000
      613.9´51—dc21   99-30167
                                            CIP

Staff Credits
Anne Heller, editor; Adam Lazar, designer; Heidi Schoof, photo researcher

Photo Credits
Cover: ©PhotoDisc/Barbara Penoyar
FPG International/©Michael Krasowitz, 30; ©Ron Chapple, 41; ©Telegraph Colour Library, 43
International Stock/©Camille Tokerud, 7; ©Mitch Diamond, 9; ©Michael Philip Mannhemi, 37; ©Clint Clemens, 53
Photo Network/©Esbin-Anderson, 10; ©Eric R. Berndt, 34; ©MacDonald Photography, 58
Photri-Microstock/©Tom and Dee Ann McCarthy, 56
Unicorn Stock Photos/©Robert Ginn, 22; ©Jeff Greenberg, 25; ©Eric R. Berndt, 27
Visuals Unlimited/©Mark E. Gibson, 33; Jeff Greenberg, 48

A 0 9 8 7 6 5 4 3 2 1

ADL-2274

Table of Contents

Chapter Overview

Part of sexuality is understanding ourselves as human beings—our body, mind, feelings, and relationships.

Sexuality begins at birth. A person's sexuality is always developing.

People of the opposite sex who are attracted to one another have a heterosexual orientation.

People of the same sex who are attracted to one another have a homosexual orientation. Usually males who have sexual relationships with other males are called gay. Females who have sexual relationships with other females are called lesbian.

Sexual harassment, assault, and abuse are all unhealthy sexual behaviors.

Chapter 1

Defining Sexuality

The word *sex* can mean many different things. It may refer to gender—being male or female. It is used to talk about reproduction, or having a baby. The desire to have sex is a popular theme in movies, on television, and in books and magazines. However, sex is more than having intercourse. Penetration of the penis into the vagina, anus, or mouth is just part of sex. Sex is just one part of a person's sexuality.

I had a great health teacher in high school. He challenged us to find good resources and learn the facts about sex and sexuality. Our final project was to write a paper defining sexuality. He gave us a homework assignment to share the paper at home with our parents.

My parents rarely talked with me about sex. So, of course, I was a little freaked out. But it turned out okay. My parents asked me some questions about my paper. I asked them a few questions, too.

I tell my friends to talk with their parents about sex. I never would have said that before. Now I know parents can be cool about it. Your parents are an important connection.
—Mandy, age 18

An important part of sexuality is how we think of ourselves as human beings. When we get to know ourselves well, we understand more about our sexuality. We grow to understand that sexuality involves the body, mind, emotions, and relationships. We learn to be comfortable with our gender and sexual orientation. Understanding sexuality can be a complicated process.

As we change and grow, so do our attitudes about sexuality. Our life will change, and so will our choices. You are in control of developing your own healthy attitudes toward sexuality. Your personal success and the success of future relationships are up to you. This book is intended to help provide an understanding of what affects your sexual development and attitudes toward sexuality.

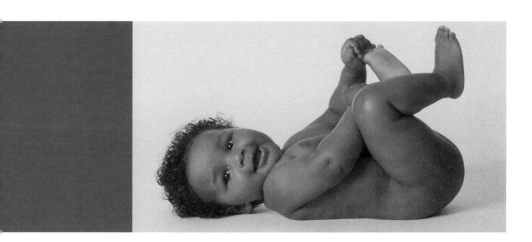

Sexuality Starts at Birth

Learning about sexuality begins at birth. From an early age, children learn names for each body part. It is helpful if they learn the correct words from the beginning. Knowing such words as *penis* and *vagina* gives children a positive understanding of their body.

Children's ideas about sexuality continually grow and change. They watch adults to see how relationships work. As they learn to speak, they model the words and sentences that adults use. Most children begin learning the language of sexuality at a very early age.

Into the Future

Imagine what your ideal self would be like in 5 or 10 years. Would your attitudes about sexuality be any different from what they are today? How would they be the same?

Children learn about their body through exploration. They discover warm sensations when touching their genitals, or sex organs. They begin to predict what feelings their body will have. In many cases, the attitudes they develop are connected to responses from adults about their explorations. For example, children who are scolded for touching their genitals may connect shame with sexuality. On the other hand, some children who ask questions may learn that the sensations they feel are normal.

As children become teens, they learn more about sexuality. They learn about defining and being comfortable with their sexual orientation. They think about choosing to have a sexual relationship. They think about when they are ready to have such a relationship and with whom. A positive, healthy understanding helps teens think about their sexuality in their own individual way and time.

Healthy Sexuality

Sexual Orientation

Sexual orientation partly defines sexuality. Sexual orientation is attractions to other people as males or females. Opposite-sex attractions are called heterosexual. In a heterosexual relationship, a male and a female are sexually attracted to one another.

Same-sex attractions are called homosexual. Males who are attracted to males are called gay. Females who are attracted to females are called lesbian.

Sometimes people may be attracted to and have sex with both males and females. This is called bisexual. Some people do not feel sexual attraction or do not have sex with others. This is called asexual.

All four orientations are normal. Heterosexual, homosexual, and bisexual couples share similar experiences. They all want intimacy, or closeness, with another person. They usually date, fall in love, and spend time with friends in much the same way.

Unhealthy Sexual Behaviors

Sometimes sexual behaviors are unhealthy. Usually in these behaviors one person becomes a victim of another. Such behaviors may include harassment, assault, or some other form of sexual abuse. Most often, exploitation occurs when one person seeks sexual satisfaction against the other person's will.

In some cases, people have had negative experiences with sex. For instance, in elementary school, some students report being sexually harassed. They may be ridiculed for some difference in the way they look or behave. Teasing and sexual name-calling affect how a child understands sexuality. The child may become afraid of dealing with sexuality honestly because of painful experiences.

Some children and teens experience sexual abuse. In some cases, these people learn to treat others as they have been treated sexually. Unless this pattern is broken, the person will not be happy. He or she may hurt others. Sometimes unlearning negative attitudes is necessary if a person is to have healthy attitudes toward sexuality.

Points to Consider

Where did you get your messages about sexuality? Were the messages mostly positive or negative? Explain.

How are homosexuality, heterosexuality, and bisexuality similar?

Name a television show that portrays an individual or a couple with a healthy attitude toward sexuality.

How could an unhealthy attitude about sexuality affect a dating relationship?

Chapter Overview

The body changes in many ways during puberty. The genitals mature until the sex organs are ready to produce or release male and female sex cells.

Sexual desire is a normal feeling that begins to appear during puberty.

Sexual intercourse includes vaginal, anal, or oral penetration.

Reproduction occurs when a male's sperm fertilizes a female's egg. Then a human life is produced from this first cell.

Chapter 2

The Human Body and Reproduction

During adolescence, the human body undergoes big changes. This time of change is known as puberty. Most of these changes occur between the ages of 9 and 17. A child's body becomes the body of a young adult during puberty. This stage prepares a young man or woman to reproduce, or be able to have a baby.

Both males and females experience changes in their body. These changes also affect an adolescent emotionally. The adolescent's body may look like that of an adult, but the mind still may be that of a child. This can be stressful. The young person often feels awkward or out of place. The changes can affect how an adolescent thinks about himself or herself. A positive attitude about sexuality can help a person feel more comfortable with these body changes.

Body Changes at Puberty

Both boys and girls experience similar body changes at puberty. Pubic hair begins to grow in the genital area. Body hair increases under the arms and on the legs. Sweat glands become active. As perspiration combines with bacteria on the skin, body odor develops. During puberty, the skin tends to get oilier. Pimples, or "zits," may be common on the face, chest, back, and neck. Usually the body goes through a series of growth spurts as it approaches full height.

An increase in hormone activity causes these changes at puberty. Hormones are chemicals that are produced throughout the body to control growth and different body functions. The hormones travel in the bloodstream. During puberty, the hormones send messages to the sex organs—a girl's ovaries and a boy's testes. The messages trigger the sex organs to produce sex hormones.

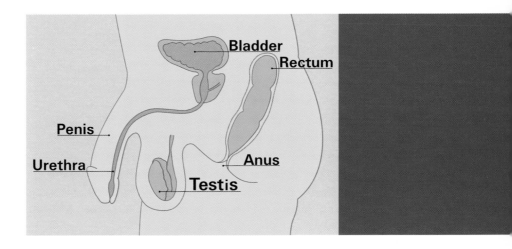

I really didn't start going through puberty until I was about 16. I was one of the smallest guys in class. I hated changing in the locker room. I worried about being weird or different.

Raymond, Age 18

My dad and I talked about my fears of never getting taller or growing to be a man. He said he started changing later than his friends did, too. My dad is a big guy, so I didn't really believe him. Nobody could say anything to make me feel better. I just kept waiting for my body to do something.

Finally, I started to notice some changes. I grew about six inches in six months. My grandma barely recognized me when she saw me. Now I'm about two inches taller than my dad is. He likes to say, "I told you so." He and I still talk about what my body is doing. All the things that happened were kind of overwhelming. I'm lucky to have my dad to talk with.

The Male Body

A boy usually begins puberty between ages 10 and 15. It takes a few years to complete the growth process. He experiences some changes that are different from a girl. For example, males may grow whiskers on their face. Also, a male's voice gets deeper.

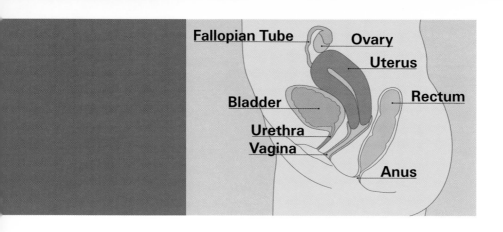

With the increase in hormones during puberty, the male's sex organs grow and begin to mature. The testes begin to produce sperm, the male sex cells, in adolescence. The testes begin to make sperm a year after puberty begins. They continue making sperm throughout life.

During sexual arousal, the penis becomes larger and hard. When ejaculation occurs, semen is suddenly released from the urethra, the long tube in the penis. Semen is a sticky, white fluid that contains the sperm. Ejaculation can happen during sleep, masturbation, or sexual activity. Masturbation is the pleasurable rubbing or touching of the sex organs.

Urine is also passed through the urethra. During sexual arousal, a valve shuts off the entry point for urine. This prevents a male from urinating at the same time he is having intercourse.

The Female Body

Girls typically begin puberty at an earlier age than boys do. Usually girls begin puberty between ages 9 and 14. Girls may be taller than boys for several years. By the time females reach their full height, however, they usually have not grown as tall as boys.

Early menstruation is often inconsistent in young women. It may take one to two years to have a regular menstrual cycle. Some girls and women's periods may never be consistent. This is perfectly normal.

An adolescent girl's hips grow wider as her body prepares for having children. A girl's breasts also begin to develop and grow.

The adolescent female body prepares for reproduction in another important way. The menstrual cycle begins during puberty. In this cycle, the ovary releases an egg, the female sex cell. Eggs are in a girl's ovaries from birth. The body doesn't continue producing them. Normally just one egg a month goes into the fallopian tube. This tube leads to the uterus, the organ in which an unborn baby grows and develops. This process is called ovulation.

Usually, the egg is not fertilized with a male's sperm. The egg then leaves the body through the vagina during menstruation. Having a period is another name for menstruation. The menstrual fluid, or menses, builds up on the lining of the uterus so that a fertilized egg could grow in it. The menses consists of blood, fluid, and tissue. When no egg is fertilized, the fluid is passed monthly over a three- to eight-day period. A menstrual cycle is about a month long.

Sexual Desire

During puberty, other changes happen. Both young men and young women begin to have romantic and sexual feelings. They have attractions to other people that are sometimes called crushes. Sexual desire becomes very strong. Often sexual desire becomes so strong that it results in sexual intercourse for adults and some teens.

Sexual desire often brings some dramatic emotional highs and lows. Intense joy and uncontrolled laughter are examples of emotional highs. Common emotional lows among adolescents are rejection or uncertainty about what to do sexually. Often these highs and lows result from attractions to other people.

Sexual Intercourse

Sexual intercourse is vaginal, anal, or oral penetration. Vaginal intercourse occurs when the penis penetrates the vagina. Anal and oral intercourse are different types of sexual penetration. The penis penetrates the anus during anal intercourse. Oral intercourse is the sucking or licking of a male's penis or a female's clitoris or vagina.

During intercourse, the penis and clitoris fill with blood and become larger. The penis is the center of sexual sensation for males. The clitoris is the center of sexual sensation for females.

Orgasm is the climax, or end, of sexual excitement. Males typically have an orgasm every time they ejaculate. Sometimes females do not have an orgasm during intercourse. Other times they may experience more than one orgasm. An orgasm can happen during masturbation or while having sexual thoughts as well as during intercourse.

Reproduction

Vaginal intercourse is the only type of intercourse from which pregnancy can result. Pregnancy also can happen when sperm are near the vagina. Fertilization of the egg happens when the sperm is united with the egg. Together the egg and sperm become the beginning cell of a human life. The fertilized egg travels to the uterus. The egg beds and grows in the built-up lining of the uterus.

The fertilized egg grows into a fetus, or unborn baby. The fetus usually grows in a woman's uterus for 38 to 42 weeks. Childbirth happens at the end of a pregnancy. A baby is born when the mother pushes the baby out of her cervix and vagina. Sometimes a baby is removed from the uterus in a surgical procedure called a cesarean section.

Points to Consider

Why do you think the human body is able to reproduce at such a young age?

What are some emotional highs and lows you experienced or are experiencing during puberty?

Why does a female have a menstrual period once a month?

Why do you think males and females often experience orgasm at different times?

Chapter Overview

A good understanding of sexuality requires accurate facts.

Parents are an excellent source of information about sexuality. Other sources of information include caring adults, health care workers, health teachers, or guidance counselors.

It is important to communicate personal beliefs and sexual boundaries to each dating partner.

Listening is a skill that takes practice and is important in any relationship.

Chapter 3

Communication and Sexuality

Puberty is an exciting process for many teens. Teens have natural curiosity and questions about the changes that puberty brings. Teens need reliable information to have sound answers to their questions and a healthy attitude about sexuality. They also need skills to communicate well and make clear decisions about sexuality.

Getting Information

Parents are a child's first teachers of sexuality. Their teaching may occur through words, actions, or body language. They also can answer questions and support their child's discoveries. Parents can provide help for teens during puberty. Teens can ask parents to share stories of how they dealt with sexuality while growing up. Parents can discuss the fears and concerns they had during adolescence. Stories about common experiences can help build a teen's relationship with his or her parents.

Some parents may not feel comfortable talking about sexuality. This can be a hard topic for some parents to discuss. When this happens, other caring adults may be able to provide accurate information and openly talk with teens. Sometimes a caring adult can discuss specific concerns or fears about sexuality more easily than a parent can. Trusted adults can be strong connections for youth. They have learned from experience many things that may help teens to adjust to the changes from childhood to adulthood.

Teens need accurate, detailed information about sexual facts. For instance, even the most caring adults may not understand sexual orientation. As a result, the adults may not have the right words or information for talking about it. Many national, state, county, or city agencies can provide help. Health care workers have the most current information. At school, health education teachers and guidance counselors can be important resources. If they can't answer your questions, they can help find a source that can provide information. In many cases, you can get free or low-cost counseling help.

Healthy Sexuality

Talking With Friends

Friends are an important part of a teen's life. They share adventures, talk of embarrassing moments, and just "hang out" together. Friends may be good listeners for painful stories. You may share hours of laughter with them. It can be very helpful to talk with your friends about sexuality. However, friends may not be the best source of information about sexuality.

Many teens report incorrect information about sexuality. This may come from misunderstanding or from getting incomplete information. Misleading facts about sex and sexuality can be dangerous. Believing such misleading facts could lead to choices that result in a sexually transmitted disease (STD) or an unintended pregnancy. False information can lead people to hurt one another unknowingly.

Myth vs. Fact

Teens often report these common myths to other teens.

Myth: You can't get pregnant standing up.

Fact: You can get pregnant any time semen enters or is near the vagina and an egg is present.

Myth: Masturbating can cause physical problems.

Fact: Masturbating is a normal part of exploring the body and will not cause any physical problems.

I have always been really shy. I never dated much until last year. Dating was hard for me at first. I never thought there would be so much pressure. When my boyfriend would start to touch my body or pressure me for sex, I would laugh. I didn't know how to tell him to slow down.

Jen, Age 17

One day I asked my dad if he dated much in high school. I wanted to know if it was normal for guys to pressure girls. He said he always talked with his girlfriends about what they were comfortable doing. He suggested I quit laughing and start talking to my boyfriend about what I wanted. Talking with my dad gave me so much confidence.

The next day my boyfriend and I talked about sex for about an hour. It turned out he was feeling pressure from his friends to have sex, and he didn't really feel ready. I definitely was not ready for sex. Our relationship is much better now. We don't let friends interfere with what we want. And I'm more confident in sharing my feelings.

Talking With a Dating Partner

Personal beliefs and sexual boundaries should be discussed with each dating partner. Couples may or may not decide to have sexual intercourse. However, it is important to talk about sex before it happens. This discussion can address the possible outcomes of a sexual relationship such as pregnancy or STDs.

It is important for dating partners to talk about whether they're ready for sexual activity. Different people have different time lines for being ready for sexual activity. This may come from a difference in their future plans. It may come from a different comfort level with certain behaviors at certain times.

Open communication is important to any relationship. It is a good idea to share past sexual history. This discussion permits the other person to know about possible risks for STDs. Partners can inform each other about what they expect from the relationship. This sort of sharing helps promote a satisfying experience for both people. If this does not happen, you may want to reevaluate the relationship. You may choose to end the relationship.

Talking with your partner about sexuality can be difficult. However, it can be even harder to talk about STDs, pregnancy, and sexual problems after they have occurred. Each person should take some time to share his or her sexual beliefs. Such communication is part of healthy sexuality.

Listening to a Partner

Listening is part of any healthy relationship, especially a healthy sexual relationship. Good listening means you can hear what a person is saying. You also can tell from the other person's face and body language things he or she may not be saying in words. Listening is one good way to show you care about someone. It may take some time to become a good listener. Like any activity worth doing, listening takes skill, practice, and patience.

Good listeners use some helpful techniques. You can practice the following techniques any time and with anyone:

Paraphrase, or restate, what the other person said. This shows you understand what the speaker said and his or her viewpoint.

Ask clarifying questions. These questions help the listener to understand what the speaker meant. Clarifying questions can help the listener understand how the speaker feels.

Pay attention to body language. Body language is unspoken, or nonverbal, messages. Examples of body language are facial expressions, arm movements, and body posture. Body language such as nods help the speaker know the listener is paying attention.

Eye contact can be a way to show you are listening. In some cultures, eye contact is not acceptable. Usually, however, it is acceptable in North America.

Healthy Sexuality

Listen "between the words" to what the person is not saying. Sometimes what people do not say is a clue to what they really mean. Sometimes when a listener shares hunches or instincts, it helps the speaker clarify his or her own meaning and feelings. Teens need to hear the tiny voice in their head. It is often instincts or "gut" feelings that help people make good decisions.

Avoid distractions. There can be many distractions to careful listening. The radio, television, or telephone can interfere or interrupt the speaker's train of thought. Turn off the TV, radio, CD player, or VCR. Let the telephone ring. If it's important, the person will call again. Listen to your partner and listen to yourself.

Points to Consider

How do parents affect a person's understanding of sexuality?

What could happen to a teen who receives false information about sexuality? Give a specific example.

What are the benefits of good communication while dating another person?

Describe some characteristics of a good listener.

Chapter Overview

Taking care of yourself sexually includes keeping your body clean.

Using protection during sexual activity helps to avoid an unwanted pregnancy or STDs.

Setting sexual limits, being assertive, and using resistance are important skills in taking care of yourself sexually.

Chapter 4

Sexual Self-Care

It is each person's job to take care of himself or herself. It is especially important to take care of yourself sexually. This includes good hygiene, or cleanliness habits. It also includes setting sexual limits. You may need to use assertiveness and resistance skills to maintain the limits you set for yourself. If you develop good self-care skills, you help to ensure your own healthy future.

Cleanliness

Good hygiene, or cleanliness, helps to avoid disease and skin problems that teens commonly have. Regular baths or showers help to eliminate perspiration and body odor. Most people find they need to wash their skin with soap and their hair with shampoo every day. Also, washing your hands frequently helps to reduce the spread of germs and disease. If you are sexually active, it is a good idea to bathe after having sex.

Deodorant can be used to cover body odor during the day. An antiperspirant can help to control sweating. Neither deodorants nor antiperspirants, however, remove bacteria that make you smell bad. Only washing with soap and water removes the bacteria. During puberty, adolescents find they may have to wash more often than they did before.

Sexual Intercourse

Taking care of your body sexually is your choice and your responsibility. One important rule is always to use protection during vaginal, anal, or oral intercourse. Vaginal, anal, or oral intercourse is safer when a condom is used consistently and properly. Condoms reduce the risk of pregnancy and STDs. Chapter 5 explains more about the need for protected sex.

Another important rule is that if some sexual activity is painful for you, don't do it. Remember that no one has the right to pressure you to do anything you don't want to do. It's your body.

In setting your sexual limits, here are some questions to ask yourself:

- Will I kiss someone using my tongue?
- What parts of my partner's body am I willing to kiss?
- Will I allow someone to touch my genitals?
- Will I take off any of my clothes?
- Am I willing to undress in the light in front of my partner?
- How will I talk about my sexual limits with my partner?

My girlfriend and I met at a party. She was making out with me and all of a sudden she said, "That's it," and left the room.

Teng, Age 18

When I found her later, she told me we had reached her limit. I wondered if I was supposed to be reading her mind. After I cooled down, we had a good conversation about sex. We didn't really start off in such a good way. Now I know where she's coming from. We both agreed we should have talked about it first.

It's not possible to know what another person is thinking. But if you talk about it, at least reaching the limit isn't some big surprise.

Healthy Sexuality

Setting Sexual Limits

A sexual limit is a boundary on sexual activity, or a point beyond which someone will not go. Each person decides what sexual activity is his or her limit. For example, one person may believe hugging and kissing is the sexual limit for him. Another person may limit sexual activity to oral sex without vaginal intercourse.

It is important to set your limits in a relationship before any sexual activity takes place. Setting sexual limits is very difficult while you are engaging in sexual activity. This is because sexual desire and attraction can be intense. They can blur your judgment and decision making.

By setting clear sexual limits, you can reduce high-pressure situations. Relationships in which the people respect one another's limits have a better chance of lasting. People are less likely to feel confused, resentful, or angry.

Being Assertive

A person needs to be assertive, or confident, when sharing sexual limits. Talking about sex can be uncomfortable for some people. However, honesty is important in taking care of yourself.

Assertive people are honest about their feelings. They are relaxed yet firm in their beliefs. They understand it is a sign of strength to talk honestly about their emotions and limits. Assertive people stand up for their rights. They express their feelings and beliefs appropriately without harming the rights of others.

When people are assertive, they show respect for themselves. They also gain respect from others. People who are assertive in sharing their sexual limits can build long-term relationships that are honest and open. They also increase their chances of feeling good about themselves.

Assertiveness works when dealing with many other situations as well. The chart may help you to determine how assertive you are.

Measure Your Assertiveness

Choose the number in each item below that best describes you.

1 = Never	3 = Sometimes 5 = Always
2 = Rarely	4 = Usually

1. I do my own thinking and make my own decisions.   1 2 3 4 5

2. I freely express my feelings and beliefs.   1 2 3 4 5

3. I accept responsibility for my life.   1 2 3 4 5

4. I make decisions and accept the consequences.   1 2 3 4 5

5. When I need help, I ask others to help me.   1 2 3 4 5

6. When at fault, I apologize.   1 2 3 4 5

7. When confused, I ask for explanation.   1 2 3 4 5

8. When someone is annoying me, I ask that person   1 2 3 4 5
   to stop.

9. When treated unfairly, I object.   1 2 3 4 5

10. I ask my doctor all the questions I want answers for.   1 2 3 4 5

11. When I am interrupted, I politely comment on the   1 2 3 4 5
    interruption and then finish what I am saying.

12. If friends invite me to do something and I really don't   1 2 3 4 5
    want to, I turn down the request.

13. When someone criticizes me, I listen to the criticism   1 2 3 4 5
    without being defensive.

14. When one friend is not meeting all my needs, I   1 2 3 4 5
    establish meaningful relationships with many other people.

15. If I am jealous, I explore the reasons for my feelings.   1 2 3 4 5
    Then I look for other ways to increase my self-confidence.

Total your score. The higher your score, the greater is your level of assertive
behavior.

Resistance Skills

Resistance is another important part of taking care of yourself sexually. Resistance or refusal skills are the ability to withstand pressure. Sexual activity, drug use, or peer pressure may require a person to use resistance skills. Resisting requires clear verbal and nonverbal messages.

Try these resistance techniques during times of pressure:

Give a clear message in a firm voice such as, "When I say no, I mean no."

Use body language to support your message. Stand straight and tall. Match your facial expression with your message.

Avoid making up reasons why you are saying no. Give no excuses, and repeat the refusal as often as necessary.

Suggest an alternative activity. If the person doesn't accept your refusal, suggest a different activity such as going for a walk.

Continue to communicate and discuss the problem. You may need to do this at a different time rather than while you are resisting. Couples who talk about limits and pressures increase their comfort and work to build their relationship.

Leave the situation if the other person or people keep pressuring you.

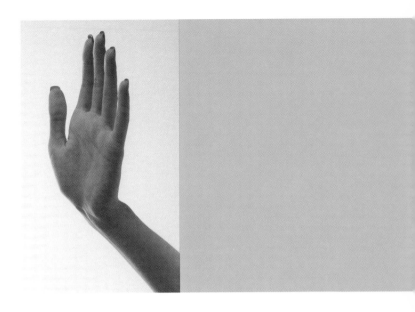

Points to Consider

What are three ways you can take care of yourself sexually?

Why do you think it would be a good idea to bathe or shower before and after sex?

Why do you think it is important to set sexual limits before engaging in sexual activity?

What are some successful resistance skills that you have used?

Chapter Overview

Pregnancy and STDs are possible consequences of having sex without using protection.

Each year three million teens get an STD.

Couples need to discuss how they would prevent pregnancy or deal with an unplanned pregnancy. Condoms are the most common choice among teens to prevent pregnancy as well as STDs.

Using protection during sex shows sexual responsibility.

Chapter 5

Sexual Responsibility

Being sexually active includes many responsibilities for both partners. The first responsibility is to engage in safer sex. This means using condoms to prevent pregnancy or the spread of STDs. Sexual responsibility also means respecting the sexual rights of others. A person who is sexually responsible doesn't commit or put up with sexual assault, sexual harassment, or sexual abuse.

Real sexual responsibility can be a challenge. People who are sexually responsible plan for pregnancy and use protection during sexual acts. They learn about STDs and how to prevent them. People who are sexually responsible do not use sex to make others victims.

When latex condoms are used correctly every time a person has sex, they:

- Are 98 percent effective in preventing pregnancy
- Are 99.9 percent effective in reducing the risk of STDs when combined with a spermicide
- Can substantially reduce the transmission of HIV

> When I was a little kid, my folks always talked about trusting me. They gave me **Greg, Age 17** responsibilities when I was really young that some kids never get. They always talked to me and listened to me, too.
>
> So by the time I was serious about a girl last year, being responsible and trustworthy was part of who I was. I knew I was going to take responsibility to be careful. I always use condoms. And I always treat my girlfriend with respect. If she says no, I respect that and don't make her go further.

Unprotected Sex

Teens face great risk when they have sex without protection. Because teens are likely to have more than one sexual partner, they are more likely to risk having unprotected sex. It is important for teens to understand this risk.

People who have unprotected sex with multiple partners have the highest risk for STDs. Also, a female's body is more likely than a male's to get an STD from unprotected sex. This is because of the way the female body is built. It has more folds and cavities inside where germs can linger and cause disease. Of course, the possibility of an unplanned pregnancy also increases with unprotected sex.

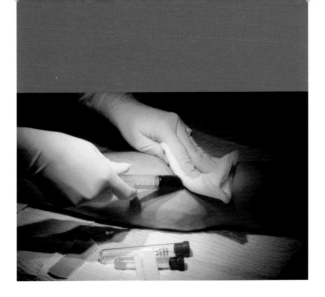

Good sexual health includes having a plan for sexual protection. A teen can choose a method to protect himself or herself. Both partners should discuss the best method together.

Sexually Transmitted Diseases

Each year three million teens acquire STDs, which often have no symptoms. Because there are often no symptoms, it is difficult to tell who is infected. Many times a person doesn't realize he or she has an STD. As a result, the person may unknowingly pass STDs to others. Early detection and treatment are important to prevent spreading infection to others.

Sexually active people should visit a health care worker regularly. The only way to be certain a person is free of disease is regular testing for STDs. People who have never had sexual relations are not carriers of STDs. They are still at risk for being infected with an STD if they become sexually active. Using latex condoms with spermicides and having regular tests effectively prevent STDs. Condoms do not prevent all types of STDs, however, because they do not cover some infected areas.

Did You Know?

Information on testing and current treatment for HIV and AIDS is available from these Centers for Disease Control hotlines:

National AIDS Hotline	1-800-342-AIDS (2437)
Spanish	1-800-344-SIDA (7432)
TTY/TTD	1-800-243-7889

Pregnancy

Some people believe that pregnancy can result only from vaginal intercourse. However, it also can result from sperm being near the vagina or entering it from the outside through underwear. Sperm swim. Therefore, it is best to keep sperm far from the vagina if a pregnancy is not planned.

When a person chooses to have sex, he or she also should think about getting pregnant or parenting. Ask yourself questions like these about your sexual partner:

Would the person make a good parent?

Would the person stay committed to our child?

Would the person be patient and loving toward me and our child?

Would the person accept adoption? Would the person accept abortion, or ending a pregnancy early?

Often the thought of sex makes everything else seem unimportant. People with an accurate view of sexuality can see all sides of the sexual experience. They talk with their partner about parenting, including how each person would handle an unplanned pregnancy. They look into the future.

Pregnancy Prevention

Sexually responsible couples plan when to start a family. They use some method to help prevent a pregnancy. Choosing not to have sex is the most effective method to prevent pregnancy.

Couples have many choices for pregnancy prevention. Women can use two methods to prevent eggs from being released or fertilized. One type of contraception is birth control pills. The other type is "the shot," which is given once every three months. Some older women use a diaphragm, which serves as a barrier to sperm. A woman must see a health care provider for all three methods.

Recently, the emergency contraceptive pill (ECP) has become widely available. This combination of pills must be used within 72 hours after unprotected intercourse. This method is not meant to be used as a regular form of contraception. A health care provider also must supply these pills.

Finally, condoms are another option to prevent pregnancy. Two types of condoms are now made. One is for males and the other for females. Male condoms are made of latex or polyurethane. They cover the penis and collect semen after ejaculation. Female condoms are bag-like pieces of polyurethane. They fit inside the vagina to prevent semen from entering the cervix. Condoms are most effective when used with spermicides.

Every sexual act should include condoms. Intercourse is 10,000 times safer with condoms than without them. Latex or polyurethane condoms are an excellent choice for preventing both pregnancy and many types of STDs. They are inexpensive and anyone can purchase them in drugstores or other stores.

Sexual Exploitation

People who are responsible about sex never use it to harm others. In some cases, teens are made victims of people producing pornography. In other circumstances, teens may be forced into prostitution. Those who are sexually responsible do not use others for their own pleasure or financial gain.

Sexual exploitation can take many forms. Pornography uses photographs of naked men, women, teens, or even children as objects, not people with personalities. Prostitution is providing sex to others for money. People who force others into prostitution usually get most of the money themselves. Sexual assault or sexual harassment uses force to show power over people. When people are only concerned with their own sexual pleasure, they exploit someone else.

Sexual harassment is a form of abuse that may include:

- Inappropriate or unwanted remarks or jokes about a person's clothing, body, sexual orientation, or behavior
- Unwanted or repeated requests or pressure for dates
- Physical behavior of a sexual nature such as patting, touching, or caressing
- Unwanted sexual requests or advances

People who experience sexual exploitation should get help. They may need to report the exploitation to law enforcement agencies in some cases. Exploitation of children and teens is unlawful. In other cases, it is important to find a safe person to talk with. This may be a parent, a counselor, a health care worker, or some trusted adult.

Points to Consider

How can someone with an STD unknowingly spread it to another person?

What future parenting qualities would you look for in a dating partner?

Name three ways to prevent pregnancy.

Why is it wrong for people to use sex to hurt or harm others?

Chapter Overview

Most teens are physically ready to have sexual intercourse at a young age. However, they may not be ready to handle the emotional side of a sexual relationship.

Couples can find sexual pleasure in ways that don't involve intercourse.

Some teens choose to abstain from sexual intercourse until a later time.

Monogamy is being in a relationship with just one person at a time. It reduces the risk of spreading STDs and shows sexual responsibility.

Chapter 6

Sexual Readiness

Most teens are physically ready to have sexual intercourse at a young age. Being emotionally ready to have a sexual relationship, however, takes more time. It can be difficult to decide whether you are personally ready to have sex. There are many factors to consider.

Is There a Right Time for Sex?

There is no magic age at which a person is ready for sexual intercourse. It takes time to define your own personal sexuality. Deciding to have sex takes careful, mature thought.

A teen must honestly answer many important questions, such as:

> Am I comfortable with my sexuality?
>
> Am I emotionally ready to handle a sexual relationship?
>
> Does it feel like the right time in my life for a sexual relationship?
>
> Have I set sexual limits for myself?
>
> Have I set standards for what I want or expect from a sexual relationship?
>
> Do I have correct information about how to prevent pregnancy and STDs?
>
> Am I ready to deal with an unplanned pregnancy?
>
> Am I ready to parent?
>
> Do I trust my partner?
>
> Can I talk with my partner about all of these things?

Self-trust and trust of the other person are vital parts of any relationship. An important part of trust in a sexual relationship is for both partners to share their sexual history. A person's sexual history may include exposure to an STD. Both partners must understand such a risk before they choose to begin a sexual relationship.

Teens worry about getting AIDS or other kinds of STDs. Four out of ten teens report being worried, at least somewhat, about getting AIDS or another STD.

I had a boyfriend for the first time in seventh grade. We spent every minute together after school. Just kissing him made me feel incredible. We got really serious real fast.

LaDonna, Age 16

We talked on the phone for hours. One night right before he said good-bye, I told him I loved him. He never said anything to me. I was crushed. I avoided him in school for the rest of the week. I couldn't believe I said it to him. But I wanted that so bad. I wanted him to love me back. I just didn't know what love was. Nobody had ever taught me.

Emotional Readiness

In a sexual relationship, the physical risks of pregnancy and transmission of STDs are very clear. However, the emotional risks in a sexual relationship may not be so clear. Couples who talk freely about all sorts of things are more likely to talk about their feelings. When they do this, they may experience intimacy.

Intimacy is the honest sharing of very personal feelings and thoughts. It is a closeness that can make sexual activity special. It can be gentle touching and caressing. Intimacy also can involve some risk taking when you share your deep personal feelings with the other person.

Unfortunately, some people are afraid to show or talk about their feelings. They may be afraid of intimacy. Some people are afraid the other person will put down their feelings. Some teens may be somewhat confused about how they feel. The hormone levels that create intense high and low feelings may increase the confusion.

Love is a strong emotion and is often confused with sexual desire. It is hard to be sure what being "in love" really is. You can love someone without sexual desire. For example, you may truly love your grandfather. This is love without sexual desire. On the other hand, you can have sexual desire for someone without loving the person.

Being ready for a sexual relationship may not mean a person is ready to show love for another. Love and sexual intercourse are not the same.

Making a Decision

Teens need to consider many factors in judging their own sexual readiness. After examining the factors, teens have many options to consider. Some teens choose to abstain from sex. Others choose alternatives to sexual intercourse. Some choose monogamy.

Abstaining From Sex

Almost all people engage in a sexual relationship at some point in their life. Many teens may feel they are ready for intimacy or even commitment to another person. However, they may choose to postpone, or delay, sexual intercourse until a later time. This is called abstinence.

My girlfriend said if I really loved her I would have sex with her. I told her that is one of the oldest lines around. I told her I loved her and I show her that love every day. I drive her to school and drop her off at the front door. I make dinner for her. I tell her I am just not ready for sex yet. I don't let her pressure me. That's the best advice I can give.
—Daniel, age 18

You may choose to abstain from sex for many reasons.

School is a priority.

You may not have met the right person.

You may choose other ways to show affection or give pleasure.

Your values or religious or personal beliefs may not support a sexual relationship at this time.

You aren't ready to have sex.

Many teens choose not to have sexual intercourse for the time being. Abstaining from sex is an effective method to avoid an unwanted pregnancy or an STD.

Alternatives to Intercourse
Sexual desire is normal. There are many healthy ways to satisfy sexual feelings without intercourse. Individually or as a couple, you can explore safe options. Two choices are masturbation and outercourse.

Masturbation is a normal part of being a sexual person. This is a healthy alternative to having sexual intercourse. It also can be a way to become comfortable with your body and to learn what pleases you sexually.

Outercourse is a way for couples to share sexual pleasures without having intercourse. They find sexual pleasure without penetration of the penis into the vagina or anus. Outercourse may include kisses, hugs, holding hands, touching, or mutual masturbation. It also may include petting above or below the waist, body rubbing, or protected oral sex.

Outercourse requires discipline, communication, and commitment. If couples aren't disciplined, outercourse can lead to vaginal or anal intercourse. Couples need to communicate in advance about using this method. They need to set what their limits will be and commit to maintaining the limits. STDs can be transmitted through oral sex. Therefore, couples still need to use some precautions such as a dental dam or flavored condom. Also, couples should be prepared with protection in case they change their mind.

Monogamy

Experimenting with sex can be exciting. Sex with many different partners may be temporarily interesting, but it involves high risk. Many people complain of a feeling of emptiness when sex does not include real intimacy.

Choosing to be monogamous is a safer choice for teens than having multiple sexual partners. Monogamy is a mutual commitment between two people. Two people who are sexually involved only with one another have a monogamous relationship. Monogamy reduces the risk of STDs and shows sexual responsibility.

Serial monogamy means each relationship has a long-term commitment. For example, Sahid dates Rosemary for eight months. Next, Sahid dates Donita for a year. During his periods of dating, Sahid only has sex with his current partner.

Points to Consider

What do you think are the three most important factors when determining readiness for a sexual relationship?

Why are emotions important in a sexual relationship?

What are some advantages of postponing sexual intercourse to an older age?

How can a couple show love for one another without having sexual intercourse?

Chapter Overview

Life experiences affect a person's definition of sexuality.

Values are the important parts of a person's life.

It is important to think carefully about the content of the media and the messages it sends about sexuality.

Each individual needs to establish his or her sexual standards within a relationship.

Chapter 7

Your Future—
Making It Work for You

Healthy sexuality is a balance of many parts of a person's life.
These include the physical and emotional parts as well as
principal relationships. This balance helps a person make
thoughtful decisions for building a healthy future. Finding this
balance and developing healthy attitudes toward sexuality take
time and commitment. Many things influence attitudes toward
sexuality, such as life experiences and messages from many
sources. A person needs time to sort out the messages.

Life Experiences

Life experiences influence a person's attitudes toward sexuality. Many teens have life experiences that help them to develop a positive view of sexuality. For others, the past may include physical or sexual abuse, assault, or negative sexual messages. These experiences and messages can hurt a person's sexual relationships. Sometimes a person needs help to overcome past experiences or erase negative messages. A counselor, therapist, or health care worker can assist people in gaining a positive attitude about sexuality.

Positive Messages

Teens can benefit from finding positive messages and role models. Parents, relatives, or neighbors can be good role models who offer positive, healthy messages. Counselors or teachers in school may be positive role models, too.

Positive messages also can come from friendships. Friends support each other. They share the same interests. They can help each other promote a healthy lifestyle. True friends don't pressure someone into something that makes the person uncomfortable. Real friends are supportive and honest.

Books can be excellent sources for positive messages. Many people write and share their personal stories about sexuality. Reading what others have experienced can positively influence your attitude about sexuality.

Understanding Messages From the Media

Buyers spend more than $100 billion a year on the media. We pay to see movies, we watch television regularly, and we buy countless magazines and newspapers. However, does the media show a healthy image of sexuality?

Almost every home in North America has at least one television set. The television is turned on an average of six hours a day. Comedies portray family and/or dating situations that promote false images of reality. Women are often shown as sex objects. These programs often reinforce negative sexual images of both men and women. Some dramatic shows combine sex and violence to tell a story. Often these stories distort what is real. Unfortunately, many young children form some of their earliest ideas about sexuality from these programs.

Many advertisers commonly use sex and attractive men and women to sell products. Most women in ads are young and thin. The advertisers seem to offer false hope to customers of having great sexual appeal if they buy a certain product.

As a consumer, or buyer, you can question the content of television, cable, film, and videos. Ask yourself these important questions about messages from the media:

Do the actors reflect the community in which I live?

Is the life of the characters realistic?

Can I find examples of healthy sexuality?

Do the characters on television and in films model healthy ways of getting along?

Films and television affect how people think about sexuality. You can be a positive consumer of media by discussing what you see with friends and family. You can live your own life rather than watching someone else live an unrealistic TV life. You can determine your own values.

Personal Values

Values are the things most important to you. Developing a healthy view of sexuality includes defining personal values.

It is important for teens to value themselves. Self-worth is a value that will help a person resist sexual pressures. Self-confidence is a value that serves as a foundation for healthy sexuality.

Most people value relationships. Sometimes people must decide if they value the relationship with or without sexual intercourse. This may happen if a partner is pressuring for sexual activity.

People who value education may choose to postpone sexual intercourse. An unplanned pregnancy would interfere with future plans for college or job training.

One value should be a set of high sexual standards.

Sexual Standards

Sex should be wonderful for both partners. This will occur only when each person defines his or her sexual standards within the relationship. Sexual standards are what a person expects and wants from sexual activity. A rewarding sexual experience requires communication, practice, and honesty between partners.

I had sex in high school. I was only in a couple of relationships, but both guys pushed my limits about sex. My younger sister starting asking me a lot of questions about sex. I was really honest with her. I told her to wait until she was older. It's hard to know what a good sexual relationship should be like when you're young. It's not worth it to start so young. I told her to wait—that it will be more meaningful later.
—Amber, age 19

Good communication is important when partners share their sexual standards. A discussion about sexual limits and expectations should happen before any sexual contact. This helps each individual understand the other person's needs.

Sexual standards help enable each person to get his or her needs met. A sexual relationship is complex. Couples constantly must talk about the strengths and weaknesses of their relationship. Through discussion, each partner can work to build a strong bond and a strong sexual experience.

Points to Consider

How have your life experiences influenced your attitudes toward sexuality?

Why does the media have such a strong impact on a person's understanding of sexuality?

Make a list of your most important values. Rank your values, with the most important being number one.

You are in a serious relationship. Your partner is trying to push you beyond your sexual limits. What would you say to the person?

Glossary

abstinence (AB-stuh-nenss)—choosing not to have sexual relations

condom (KON-duhm)—device that fits over the penis or inside the vagina; condoms prevent sperm from entering the uterus and the spread of sexually transmitted diseases.

contraception (KON-truh-SEP-shuhn)—a method to prevent pregnancy

egg (EG)—the female reproductive cell; when fertilized with a male sperm, an egg develops into a new human being.

ejaculation (ee-JAK-yoo-LAY-shuhn)—the release of semen from the penis during the peak of male sexual arousal

genitals (JEN-i-tulz)—sex organs; the male sex organ is the penis, and the female sex organ is the clitoris.

hormone (HOR-mohn)—a chemical that controls a body function

infertile (in-FUR-tuhl)—unable to reproduce, or have a baby

menstruation (men-stroo-AY-shuhn)—the monthly discharge of blood, fluids, and tissue from the uterus in nonpregnant females

monogamy (muh-NOG-uh-mee)—a sexual relationship between only two people and no one else

ovaries (OH-vur-eez)—the female organs that contain eggs

semen (SEE-muhn)—white, sticky fluid released from the testes that contains sperm

sexual intercourse (SEK-shoo-wuhl IN-tur-korss)—penetration of the penis into the vagina, anus, or mouth

sperm (SPURM)—a male reproductive cell that is capable of fertilizing a female's egg

spermicide (SPURM-uh-side)—a substance that kills sperm

testes (TESS-teez)—the male organs that produce sperm; also called testicles.

For More Information

Abner, Alison, and Linda Villarosa. *Finding Our Way: The Teen Girls' Survival Guide.* New York: Harperperennial Library, 1995.

Basso, Michael J. *The Underground Guide to Teenage Sexuality: An Essential Handbook for Today's Teens and Parents.* Minneapolis: Fairview Press, 1997.

Bell, Ruth. *Changing Bodies, Changing Lives: A Book for Teens on Sex and Relationships.* New York: Times Books, 1998.

Shields, Abby. *Little Bits of Wisdom: Tips to Survive the Teenage Years.* Mandeville, LA: ASC Publishing, 1996.

Theisen, Michael. *Sexuality: Challenges & Choices.* Winona, MN: St. Mary's Press, 1996.

Useful Addresses and Internet Sites

AIDS Foundation of Canada
885 Dunsmuir Street, Suite 1000
Vancouver, BC V6C 2T6
CANADA
www.aidsfoundation.ca

Alan Guttmacher Institute
120 Wall Street
New York, NY 10005
www.agi-usa.org

Kaiser Family Foundation
2400 Sand Hill Road
Menlo Park, CA 94025
www.kff.org/archive/repro

Planned Parenthood Federation of America
810 Seventh Avenue
New York, NY 10019
1-800-669-0156
www.plannedparenthood.org

Planned Parenthood Federation of Canada
1 Nicholas Street, Suite 430
Ottawa, ON K1N 7B7
CANADA
www.ppfc.ca

Adolescence Directory On-Line
www.education.indiana.edu/cas/adol/adol.html
Information on adolescent issues

Kids Help Hotline in Canada
kidshelp.sympatico.ca/help/index.htm
Information and tips on friendship, love, birth
control, AIDS, abuse, sexual violence, and
more

The National Clearinghouse for Alcohol and
Drug Information
www.health.org/pubs/qdocs/index
On-line publications on drugs, HIV, and more

Sexuality Education Resource Centre
Manitoba, Inc.
www.serc.mb.ca
Facts about sexuality

teenwire
www.teenwire.com
Sexuality and relationship information for
teens

Index